Russell was born in 1981 in the Royal Sussex County Hospital in Brighton and grew up on a Council estate in Peacehaven. He had a challenging childhood as he could see and sense spirits but nobody knew what to do about it. He worked in a few different careers from Car Mechanics to delivering Cash and Valuables. Throughout different stages of his life he has continued to receive information beyond the normal senses and didn't know why.

Dedication

I would like to dedicate this book to my nana Gladys
Sawyers who over the years had been continuously
prompting me to produce a book

Russell Wilson

AND THEN THEY FOUND ME

AUSTIN MACAULEY PUBLISHERS™

LONDON • CAMBRIDGE • NEW YORK • SHARJAH

A CIP catalogue record for this title is available from the British Library.

ISBN 9781787104815 (Paperback)
ISBN 9781787104822 (E-Book)

www.austinmacauley.com

First Published (2018)
Austin Macauley Publishers Ltd.
25 Canada Square
Canary Wharf
London
E14 5LQ

Acknowledgments

Thank you very much to my Partner Tasha Wilson for helping me and supporting me along this journey

I would like to give a special thanks to Sian French, for believing in my vision and making this book possible.

Chapter 1

So it's my Thirtieth birthday. This was the one that I had waited a long time for. Thirty years in fact. I had always felt that this was the age of adulthood. Finally, the older generation would actually want to listen to me, to see what I had learnt on my journey so far. My input would now be taken seriously and I would feel understood and not brushed off. As for the younger people they would be in a hurry to know what was it like at eighteen & twenty-one, eagerly awaiting knowledge of girls, partying, and boring jobs filled with funny stories. In my younger years I had partied, very hard in fact. I had experimented with drugs, listened to dance music, stayed up all night and reached for the lasers. During these younger years I always thought that thirty was the time I leave all that behind me, no more up all night stuff, that would be it, done.

During my twenties I had planned that my thirtieth birthday cake would be different in order for me to remember this occasion forever. All my other birthdays had just been the normal or uncelebrated, so thirty had to be a good one. My plan was a big chocolate cake filled with marijuana. During my twenties normally things I had planned either didn't work out or I gave up on them. Therefore, I was very pleased with myself as I sat there aged thirty biting into a chocolate cake filled with marijuana. For some reason this turned out to be a very different experience to what I was used you. In my twenties I was a very regular marijuana user and it had never given me any problems before, partly because over time you build up a tolerance to the drug. I've had the giggles, I've laid back listening to chill out music and felt the sensation of floating over my physical body but nothing had prepared me for this. So it took its time as was expected when you eat it, during that time I was in the car with my partner and she was driving me into Brighton to meet up with my best friend and his partner. Once I got there I gave him some cake and then we went to the pub. After some time I could feel it coming on, it was like somebody was walking up behind me and then before I knew it, it had me. I burst out laughing to the point of no return, I didn't mind laughing out loud, I'm not a shy person and because we were in a busy pub my outburst went by unnoticed, but then the cake just kept going. Soon my vision was starting to go blurry and I said to my friend that I was off now and me and my partner headed home. I knew that I was done for. The drive home seemed long and something different was happening inside my brain. As we arrived home I sat on the sofa and my consciousness kept shifting me to different places within my home. It was like I kept travelling at speed through black holes and then I would appear in a different room, then I would arrive back on the sofa in my physical body. It was all a bit too much and I was ready for it to stop, after a few hours it did finally slow down. Clearly I had been over excited when mixing the ingredients. Nevertheless, morning came and I awoke filled with a sense of achievement that I had in fact done it, I had achieved my goal. Happy Birthday Russell!

Now while I had finally achieved something that I had set in motion years ago, my thirties was about to put me through a massive test. It would be a test of strength, will, emotion, heartbreak, courage, and finding my true self, the real me. I had a Court case that was due to end, this was a terrible battle at the Child Courts. I had left a relationship a few years before my thirtieth and I was trying to see my son. I had been dragged through the dirt on this and every corner of my life had been exposed and tested on. I fell out with my family and moved away. Yes, my lifestyle before that time was at the opposite ends of parenthood, I had tried to party it all out of my system before my son arrived. I had achieved this, and was on the road of being clean, but being clean brought with it its own problems. I finally saw everything with fresh eyes and could see that the drugs had hid the real reality from me. I had relationship problems that were not going to go away, and here I am with my son who's all brand new and I've got to walk away from it all. So I walked and I battled all I could to see him. I held on, stayed clean and proved myself against all the odds. However, this wasn't enough and I was cornered into giving him up.

I remember saying to myself I have two choices; either never get into another relationship again, or brush myself off and try again. Now I knew at that time that my system was telling me that there was no way I could deal with any more pain but I decided to give life another go. No more suppressing myself, a real relationship with honest feelings and honest love. I brushed myself off and went for it. I started a relationship with a girl that I had once kissed aged four in the school playground. We were at the same schools all the way through our learning years and whilst I had never told her back then, the truth was I had always liked her. We were together for some time and by the time we had both reached age thirty she wanted a baby. At that time, I didn't feel ready because of all the other things going on in my life, but I did the age calculation thing, you know, how old would the baby be when I'm forty-five etc and I decided that now would be the right age to have a baby. So here we were thirty years old and pregnant with our baby boy.

During the pregnancy I was thinking more and more about my son that I had left behind with my ex-partner. I had always been great with children over the years and always knew that I would be a great father someday and yet here I was riddled with guilt that I was about to raise one child without raising the other. It wasn't me and I hated every part of myself for it. Psychologically I started to struggle, myself care diminished and before I knew it I started to suppress this inner pain with drugs again. Now I didn't last long on the drugs this time as I had already got all of that out of my system earlier, so this time it wasn't psychologically aiding me as it used to do, it wasn't propping me up, it was just making everything seem more ugly. There was no fun to be had in it either, after all it couldn't teach me anything new, it didn't help me escape and it didn't fill the void that I had in my heart.

Over the years from a very early age I had frequently battled with lots of depression in my life. I had been clear of it for a few years, mainly because I had been suppressing and supporting myself through self-medication however during this period in my life it was all starting to work its way back in again and I didn't hold anymore methods to stop it. So I began to live with it again, I carried it around with me and used it to fill the hole that I had inside myself. Eventually it started to impact more than just my mental health, my physical health would start to suffer also. At that time I was working full time at a job that I had been in for years. I had always been employed ever since I left school aged sixteen. I was a very hard worker and always tried to make the work environment fun for everybody. I was the joker, the energiser, the ear that would always listen to you and understand without judgment. I loved everybody and sometimes hid my sensitivity behind my jokey outwardly play. So of course when my depression returned everybody could immediately see that something was clearly wrong. While I had tried to hide my feelings I didn't hide what was happening in my life. I openly told my work colleagues that I wasn't seeing my son anymore. I had gone from being the outgoing happy, funny, expressive person to a very quiet non-joking person. This new quietness stayed for months and my work colleagues began to forget about the old me. I faded away becoming just an ordinary worker disappearing into the work force. My boss started to push more work on me and because I wasn't speaking up anymore the work load just kept on increasing. I had enough to deal with, with my own personal problems that were affecting me outside of work and now with this ever increasing work load on top of that, mentally and physically I was stretched to my limit and I began to develop walking problems and increasing amounts of pain. Now while I've had back pain from the age of sixteen, I hadn't found there to be a problem with my walking before. I was born with psoriasis and had a swollen big toe on my left foot since the age of twelve. I had lied on the application form for this job and said that I didn't have any medical complaints as I really needed the job. My job involved a lot of walking and movement as there was a lot of lifting to be done but I didn't expect there to be any problems, after all I had been living with my illness all of my life. It was a highly stressful job as there was huge pressure to arrive to places at specific times and always the possibility of a physical attack. Because of my depression and this increasing work load, and now these physical problems I finally couldn't take any more of it. For the first time in my life I quit my job. My new partner is pregnant, I have rent to pay, debts to pay, bills etc, and I can't cope. I chuck it all in and leave work not knowing what will come next.

I entered a world that I had never known. I had to sign on to receive benefits. We didn't receive any money for eight weeks and we had to rely on my partners grandparents to feed us. Before long my phone was ringing with people wanting money from me. My bills had started to go to final demands and were now turning red. It felt like everybody was trying to get hold of me and here I was physically and mentally broken. I decided that I was going to have to sell my car just to pay off some bills. After I did that I had to contact a company so I could declare myself bankrupt, I had lost it all.

I had been seeing my dad again for a while when all this was happening. My dad wasn't always a part of my life, I had dipped in and out of his life on and off over the years. My soul had always felt like it was being torn in two different directions. This was probably due to the fact that I hadn't grown up with him and that in my heart I had felt him leave when I was just a few months old. I could always feel this spiritual connection towards him, this soul bond. Anyway, I had decided to make contact once again and was currently in his life once more. Now that I was older I had sworn to myself that I would stay in his life forever this time, enough messing about, set my emotions aside and just be there. Now the thing with my dad is, like some people he had a few habits. He, like myself at that time, smoked tobacco and drank alcohol. His drinking to him though was his cushion against the world, his fun, his friend, his precious. Now that I wasn't working anymore I thought this was the perfect time to get to know my dad properly. Previously I had only been popping in fleetingly as I would pass by on my home from work. So we started meeting up regularly, the pub was his daily routine, so it was at the pub where we would meet up and drink.

With what was going on in my life, drinking probably wasn't the best idea. Well I did it anyway. Dad paid as I didn't have a job and we drank, lots. We laughed, we joked, we swapped stories and we bonded. The drink was also stopping the physical pains that I had been having, it was also lifting my spirits and helping me forget about being depressed. However outside of that environment it was a different story. My son had been born and I should have been spending more time at home. Nevertheless, the pub thing continued and after sometime I was starting to creep up to my thirty first birthday.

Chapter 2

So it's my birthday again! Aged Thirty-One Happy Birthday Russell.

This was to be another trying year; I still wasn't well in my mind or my body. I was showing everybody a false face, the kind where you smile but inside you're buried deep under rubble. I was still drinking with dad which was causing friction at home, because I was out all day and would come home drunk. It all felt strange with not being at work, no routine, no time to be places, too much time to think about the past and a doomed future. I had a newly born son at home and a partner that needed me there. Here I was so focused on getting to know my dad and numbing my own pain and emotions that I was beginning to let everything else suffer in the process. I was drinking way too much and too often and I would become so drunk that I couldn't eat dinner when I would arrive home. I was meeting dad nearly every day at the pub and regularly missing meals. We would smoke and drink to numb past pains, forget about the future, and blur out the now. I quickly learned that my dad was an alcoholic and I was beginning to turn into one also. What was I doing I thought to myself, I had it all to play for, a good relationship, a lovely son at home. Yet here I am so focused on knowing my dad and numbing my own pain that I end up shadowing him in his life. If I came into the pub and ordered a soft drink he would say, "You're no son of mine". You see, Alcohol was acceptance and if I didn't drink I wouldn't be accepted. I started to see the real picture and thought about cutting and running, as this wasn't going to help me in the long run. My intuition told me to leave but I remembered that I had promised to myself that I would stay in his life for good this time no matter what, so I wasn't going to go anywhere. So I hung on it there and continued to get drunk. It wasn't long though when the worst thing that could have ever happened, happened.

From the start I could see that dad was very very thin and knew that it was the drink and lifestyle that was keeping him looking this way. He told me he had a hospital appointment and he asked me if I could go with him. I hadn't expected anything to be out of the ordinary so I agreed to go. As we sat there waiting at the hospital he kept looking at the time on his wrist watch, thinking to himself that the pub had opened and he was missing out. We watched people at the hospital go in before us and I tried to cure his boredom with showing him some stories in the newspaper, however he was soon to be called in. He told me to wait outside, we had agreed that he would call for me if he needed my assistance. A few minutes had passed and the consultant called me into the room. As I walked in I saw my dad sitting in the chair looking white as a ghost and staring at the floor. He couldn't look me in the eye. I asked the consultant what's the problem and they told me he had leukaemia. Instantly my head felt like it had exploded and suddenly my ears filled with white noise and my heart sank. They told me that I was to listen to the information so that I could tell dad at a later stage as he will probably not remember given the circumstances he is now under. The consultant spoke to us about it all, but we didn't really hear anything over the shock, we nodded and said that we understood because we wanted to leave straight away so we took his leaflets and got up out of our seats and left the hospital. My dad was broken and confused, scared and instantly felt isolated from everybody. He reached for his tobacco and attempted to roll up but his hands were shaking so much that he couldn't roll it so I did it for him. A few words are exchanged and its decided, we are going straight to the pub. As we walk towards the bus stop he's confused and wondering how long he's got left to live. I was thinking, great I've just got to know my dad and now he's going to die. It was a bitter pill to swallow. The bus arrives and we head straight to the pub to drink over the news and forget he was ever diagnosed.

The next few months were not to be easy by any means. I went with dad to his appointments, we would go into this room at Brighton hospital where all these people are connected to IV's all pumping different things into their bodies. Dad was receiving platelets and some injections into his stomach. My dad was a joker and would say funny things to the nurses while he was receiving his treatments. We were also required to travel up to London for some of the appointments. This journey used to really take his toll on him as we would have to take a bus ride and then two trains to get there. When you are dying of cancer battling with long distance public transport is the last thing that you need in your life. He didn't always tell me what these appointments were for, he was probably emotionally protecting me. I do know, however some of the appointments were to receive a bone marrow biopsy. It was an invasive process where they drill a hole into your hip bone and extract the marrow. He was so brave and I loved him even more for it. I would try to make the journey seem less daunting by trying to amuse him in conversation, it didn't ever work though. He used to be lost in thought with his attention drawn to looking out of the window on the train. I once decided to wrap two ice cold beers in a towel and sneakily bring them up to London with me so after his appointment he could have a beer before the long journey home. Dad was amazed as I pulled these two beers out of my bag and sure enough they were still chilled. I was with him nearly every day and by this point we would now start at the pub and then we would continue to drink at his home. We talked a lot about death and what it might be like. Where he might be when it would happen. He used to joke that he would be sitting in the armchair with his trousers around his ankles and his feet in a washing up bowl filled with porridge with a dirty magazine on his lap. He giggled and said imagine the ambulance crew having to explain that one. The thing is though when you have been told you don't have long to live you do start to question when will it come, can it be stopped, how do you live with a sell by date. Truth is we all have a sell by date, we just don't know when that date is. I looked for cures all over the internet to try and gather as much information as I could find. There was lots of information about treating cancer with cannabis. We decided to not treat the cancer with cannabis as cannabis is still illegal in the UK therefore getting hold of what he would need regularly would impose great problems. So we carried on going to the pub and messing around like teenagers. After about eight months the hospital appointments were beginning to take their toll on Dad and his mental health was now declining quicker than his physical health. It was a struggle to talk about anything else other than his diagnosis, not just for me but for everyone, the small talk seemed to be fading. How could anybody ask if he was alright, the look on his face gave you the answer before you could even ask the question. The diagnosis had changed everything. It was very sad to see and with that sadness it started to pull me under even more. I tried to resist being pulled under as I was supposed to be his rock I couldn't last though and I was crushed in the end. I decided that I needed to start medicating, not alcohol, not street drugs but real prescribed medication. I booked to see the doctor and started a course of antidepressants. I didn't want to tell dad about this as he would of thought of me as being weak so I kept it hidden from him. These new tablets were about to cause problems though as the leaflet says no alcohol. So I tried to reduce the days that I was at the pub and that way I would still drink when I saw dad so he wouldn't know. This quickly became a problem though as I guess dad thought I didn't want to be around him anymore as I now wasn't in the pub every day. I was still accompanying dad to most of his appointments but not all of them, I was also trying to keep everything sweet at home too, However these tablets were adjusting me psychologically and emotionally and this was making communication harder. After a few months

I had fully numbed how I felt emotionally and therefore I found expressing myself to be much harder. Mentally though I felt much happier that my emotions were now numb to it all, but I didn't like the new anxiety that I was beginning to experience with these tablets. I noticed an increased heart rate and bigger pupils, it was to be expected as these tablets were SSRI's which is a selective serotonin reuptake inhibitor. On the days that I was drinking at the pub I would retreat and sit in the corner as I was experiencing bouts of anxiety. I would watch my dad talk to other people pretending that he was fine. I felt like I couldn't handle any of these people anymore, I was struggling to handle the lack of honesty between them all. They were alcoholics and I felt that they would corrupt my dad into drinking more and more. I felt disconnected and I could no longer relate to anyone. I had to get out of there.

After sometime on these tablets, I started to get an increasing pain in my lower back and I began to develop some more severe problems with my walking. My legs would now sometimes go from under me as I would walk, my heart was pounding faster than normal, and I felt completely different. I had lost all concept of time. I started to stay at home more and told dad that I was having walking problems, he said to me that when I'm well, to come down to the pub. I went down a few times off and on but found my mobility to be getting worse and worse, in the end I found that I couldn't make it down to the pub anymore on foot. So I started to get driven down there, my anxiety was making me sweat a lot so now I was becoming body conscious which in turn made my anxiety worse. I would sit shaking in the corner and force myself to drink at least one pint and then make excuses and leave. Dad was still having treatment and was now going on his own as I was too ill to walk with him to his appointments. The relationship was beginning to break down.

My partner decided to take me to the doctors. I waited to be called and told the doctor about my back pain and the walking problems that I was having. The doctor did a few tests and then took a deep breath and said, "Oh dear I think you have Psoriatic Arthritis". The doctor told me that somebody in her family has it and it is a very painful condition, so expect pain from now on. Great I thought. Now I knew that I was born with psoriasis and I knew that my big toe on my left foot had swelling in it from the age of twelve, but I had honestly forgotten about it, I had learned to live with it and I felt that I was in control. So the doctor referred me to a specialist for more tests. My referral was to take some weeks and if I needed anything in the meantime then I was to come straight back to the doctors. As the weeks passed my pain got worse, I didn't make it to the pub and dad didn't come to my home to see me. He still went to his treatments and we would talk over the phone.

Myself and my partner eventually got the specialist appointment date and off to the hospital I went for tests. They took blood, x-rayed my hands, chest, feet, ankles, and I was scanned using the MRI machine. After the tests I was free to go home and was to wait for the next appointment where I would receive the results. During this waiting time I had started to eat my way through various painkillers and was now having bouts of sciatica. The date for the results came and off to the hospital we went. The results were: Psoriatic Arthritis, HLA-B27+, Sacro-Ileitis, Ankylosing Spondylitis, pain similar to Fibromyalgia, and nail dystrophy. She also told me it was environmental factors beyond my control that would contribute to my illness. I remember thinking that's a bit of a long list. I was told that in about eight month's time I will never be able to walk again. Here I was thinking how am I going to kick a ball with my son, how will I be there for dad, what use will I be to my partner and will she leave me after all the stuff I've been through with dad. Everything was caving in, I had loads of questions.

I was offered a treatment program of medication to try and slow my disease down but warned there are side effects and no guarantee of a result. I thought of my family and said yes, let's go for it. I was prescribed Methotrexate and Etanercept. I am told that I will have to attend my doctors regularly to do blood tests; this was so they could count my white blood cells as the methotrexate was meant to reduce the number of them. A little book to monitor my methotrexate doses and my Etanercept was to be delivered to me at home as it needed to stay at a certain temperature. Methotrexate was to be taken orally and Etanercept was self-injection. I wasn't looking forward to any of it at all. Methotrexate was weekly for one year and Etanercept was weekly also for two years.

I went to the pharmacy to collect my Methotrexate and my Etanercept was due to be delivered to my home. My Etanercept arrives and it's time to start the treatment. I take a couple of Methotrexate pills as they are in low doses, it's a precautionary method so you don't overdose on them accidentally. I then move into the lounge where I sit down looking at this injection. Now the injection comes in a pre-filled pen system. The needle is spring-loaded and the 50mil Etanercept is already inside, there are two possible injection sites according to the instructions. Option one, inject into your triceps, back of upper arm. Option two, your thigh. Now these injections have to go into muscle and not a direct vein, so I sit looking at my arm, I pinch the back of my upper arm as a test to see how bad the sting is. It stung a bit and I was also thinking that because I'm not a big guy, there really isn't much to inject into back there, besides it's not easy to see what I'm doing there either. So it was to be the thigh. I inspect this pen injection further, my hands were sweating and my heart was racing. It had a button at the top, and a safety cap at the base. I look down at my legs, and choose a leg, I then used the alcohol wipe to clean the area and start psyching myself up ready to inject. I remove the safety cap and press the pen against my thigh, I make a few panic noises and take a deep breath and click! Nothing happened, the pen jammed! So now I have to go through all that psychological build up again. I put it back to my leg and click! Still not gone. Now by this time I'm ready to give it up, I'm all hot, heart racing and feeling light headed. Out of frustration and with some anger I put it aggressively against my leg said to my partner, this fucking thing doesn't work and I pushed the button, and boom the needle drops into my leg and then the pen clicks and in the little inspection window all the liquid had gone. Well that's it I said, I've poisoned myself, let's hope the body is fine with it. While I was calming down I was questioning whether I could survive my next self-injection in a week's time.

During that week I wasn't too aware of any changes apart from now dreading my next injection day. I needed to take my mind off it and wanted to see dad to talk about it all. So where was dad, well naturally I was going to have to go to the pub. Now there where strict guidelines about the Methotrexate and one of them was no alcohol, and here I am on my way to the pub to see my dad. I managed to walk to the pub and I said to myself along the way, oh well it's not a problem I will just drink orange juice with lemonade. So I arrived at the pub, dad's sitting in his regular chair which just so happens to be a stall at the bar, right next to the beer taps. I hug him, tell him I've missed him and pull up a seat. What you having dad said, I said it's alright I've got this, as I just knew that what I was about to order wasn't going to sit well with him. Orange juice with lemonade I asked the bar tender, it's all fine with the bar tender and my drink is being poured. The look coming off dad was a disapproving look, and he said you aren't no son of mine drinking that. I thought thanks dad, I've only come in here to see you and as you're here every single day of the week how else will I see get to see you?

So we start talking and I ask how he's been doing, he had been juggling doctors, hospital and pub. He was having chemo and drinking all the way through his treatments, he was thinner but seemed to be coping mentally now. I told him about my new treatments and it seemed like we had lots in common as we were both back and forward to the hospital and doctors. Dad said that there wasn't anything wrong with me and I should stop taking my medication. I was unsure at the time so I decided to continue with my treatments. We kept talking and I was trying to make my drink last as long as I could and I could see dad looking at it going down, he kept saying leave that and I will get you a proper drink. I told him I couldn't drink due to the medication. He disapproved as he was drinking during his treatments and he was fine, so after a bit of pressure I buckle and get a pint. I arrive home drunk.

This went on a few times as I had now convinced myself that maybe dad was right, so while I was at the start of my treatments and on a low dose I was drinking a few times at the pub with dad again.

Chapter 3

Thirty-two comes around Happy Birthday Russell.

This year was to be about truths and heart break.

So let's sum it all up. I was on anti-depressants, I smoke tobacco, drink, took Methotrexate, Etanercept, and now and then strong pain killers, not the type you get without a prescription and to top all that I was still trying to see my dad in the pub environment.

My walking problems were getting more aggressive but I was determined to walk to the pub as I wanted to see my dad so much as I didn't know how long he had got left to live. By this time I'm now having to stop for short periods and take to sitting on residents' walls or sitting on the kerb of the road to gain enough strength to make the journey. Psychologically I had now become a mess,

I remember trying to cross the roads that were on the way to the pub and although the road was clear and free from cars, for some reason all I could see was cars. I knew they weren't there but this was confusing and I didn't really know what was happening. I was having problems with my vision as all I could see was a lot of bright light blocking what I was trying to focus on. The Methotrexate took away appetite and I was filling up on a few pints at lunchtime instead of food. My Methotrexate doses had increased but I had convinced myself that they were still low so it would be alright. The results from a recent blood test came back fine, however my methotrexate dose was due to increase soon. The injection of the Etanercept still wasn't pleasant and I was constantly dreading when the next injection was due. The pre-filled pen system was always playing me up as it didn't always fire when it was supposed to, but at least I was still doing it I thought.

The dose was raised and I was starting to not enjoy going to the pub or being around my dad because I felt so unwell. I was having headaches, all over body pain, bad stomach and a sense of confusion I was told all this was normal as my medication were doing their job. Dad was still mocking me if I ordered a soft drink in the pub, and now that I wasn't feeling well it really started to affect me emotionally. I didn't have any strength left for his banter. I thought how rude are you, I was willing to accept his habit and he's being off with me because I can't drink due to being ill. I was starting to see things as they really were, it was always all about him and seen as I had never planned on becoming an alcoholic this relationship was beginning to fade.

I began arriving at the pub later and less often again and I would return home earlier and earlier. I remember walking down there once struggling physically and in my mind feeling sad that all my dad really loves is the pub and his drink. I thought to myself well it's all my own fault really, if I had expressed myself honestly in the very beginning this relationship wouldn't have lasted longer than a week. I remembered that I had sworn to myself that I would be 100% genuine this time around, especially that I was older and yet I had failed, again. Because I wanted to know him, I tried too hard. Because I wanted to love him, I forgave too much. Because I wanted to be around him, I gave in. Because I wanted to understand him, I fused to his lifestyle. Of course all this was bound to be bad for my mental and for my physical health. I had no need to drink every day; drink didn't mean anything to me as I had already partied hard when I was younger. I hadn't been honest with myself in order to understand him, in order to know him. I started to lose sense of self and with the medication at the same time I was losing sight of who I was. I was walking home from the pub one day struggling to see properly and bam! All of a sudden, I had this pain hit me in the face, right behind my left eyeball, this pain spread to the top of my skull, it was excruciating and I thought to myself oh my god I think I am having a stroke. I was filled with panic and thought to myself if I can just make it home it will all be alright. Thankfully I did make it home that day, but the pain didn't go away for some time. I assumed it was just the medication fighting off the psoriasis and reducing the inflammation that I had. My dose had increased so I was expecting some changes so I was willing to keep going. No pain no gain. After that my Methotrexate dosing days were becoming nasty. Every time I took the pills I would be stuck indoors laying on the floor in a ball screaming with pain. I would tell my partner to take our son over to her nan's and stay there for a few hours until these pains would die down a bit. This was to now become a regular thing, I take my pills and curl up in a ball screaming for about two hours and to top it off my doses were always increasing. Now that I had reached a higher dose I decided to not drink alcohol anymore and I was spending a lot more of my time at home. It wasn't long before problems arose with my blood count, the doctors phoned me in a panic and said to stop taking the Methotrexate immediately as my white blood cell count is too low and I was at risk of death. I was instructed to wait until I had had another blood test before I would take my next dose. Great I thought, like I really need this on top of everything that's happening in my life right now. I'm now panicking that I might die and leave my partner and son behind. After a week of waiting my blood tests must have been safe as they put me back on the Methotrexate again.

I wasn't feeling any better though, my vision was getting worse, and I was becoming more confused. Walking had taken a bad turn also and my legs had finally given up. I mean they had really given up this time, there was no more limping from place to place, this was it game over. While I was at home I suddenly had lots of pain and had to lay down quick on the lounge floor I was unable to move. The pain was so strong that I was shaking all over and trying not to pass out. I had got these sharp stabbing pains running down my spine and across my bum cheeks. This was the Ankylosing Spondylitis and the Sacro-ileitis that I had been diagnosed with. I called it double sciatica and had labelled it that my walking suspension was broken. I was rolling around the floor desperately trying to find a position to get comfortable even if it was just for a second as it was taking my breath away. I was making these awful noises that sounded like a young pig in distress, and I was huffing and puffing. My partner was laughing because of these noises which in turn was making me laugh too. This was then setting my sciatica off again and I would continue to roll around the floor squealing like a pig. Now I've never been one to worry about pain much as I had always had a high pain threshold, but this was a different animal. We called the doctor. It was a giggle when he turned up I was flat on my face on the lounge floor unable to move, I said I would get up and say hello but I can't actually move at all. He asked me what was going on so I gave him all the details. He was a really lovely doctor and I felt he really understood me. He prescribed me some medication to try and help with the pain and told me to stay on them until the pain got better.

Well the pain didn't ever get any better and I kept having bouts of sciatica on and off, my stomach felt sick due to all the pills I was eating and my vision was still all over the place. I wasn't going to the pub anymore as my doses were now too high. Besides I was in too much pain to walk down to the pub by now, and I wouldn't have been able to sit upright in a chair either. I was staying at home a lot, just lying on cushions on the lounge floor watching films all day and trying to keep sciatica at bay. I invited my dad up to my home as I couldn't get to the pub but he wasn't interested by this point. I couldn't blame him really, he was thinking he might die because of his leukaemia and what do you do if you think you might die, well you do what you enjoy as much as you can and he enjoys the pub. So be it, there was my heart break, he chose the pub over me. Oh well.

Typically I had ongoing problems with the methotrexate as my blood count kept going too low, and the doctors must of phoned me on three separate occasions to put the frighteners on me, and tell me to stop taking the medication for a week as my blood count has fallen too low again. So it was on and off the medication for a bit and doing lots of blood tests. Now I didn't mind being off the medication as I always felt better in my stomach and in my head when off them, but each time going back on them was getting harder and harder, I had a specialist appointment coming up at the hospital and I was really looking forward as to what the outcome would be as I really didn't want to take these tablets or the injection anymore. The appointment arrived and on the plus side, I was told it's not worth me staying on this medication as they couldn't slow my psoriasis down and the side effects were too much. I wasn't surprised, as I was born with psoriasis which was very rare, so the disease had been running wild for years before anybody tried to slow it down, so it was too little too late. I was going to have to continue to live with it and get prepared for a wheelchair lifestyle. So me and my partner ordered a wheelchair.

One evening whilst lying in bed something popped. It was down the right side of my body around my collar bone area, it affected my heart and my jaw and I couldn't move my right arm at all. I got out of bed and went to look for any visible signs using the mirror on the hall wall. I could see that a vein was under a lot of pressure up the right hand side of my neck going behind my collar bone. So me being me. I poked it a bit as I thought that was the cause of me not being able to feel my right arm, and within a flash my heart stopped, it then did about three beats and then started to beat irregular and then my body went into a fit. I was aware and conscious about what was going on but couldn't stop my body from fitting. I hadn't ever experienced anything like this in my life before and I was now panicking as to what was going on with my body. My partner jumped out of bed and rushed to my side and with one deep breath I said call an ambulance right now! She called them and they were on their way. While we were waiting my partner was getting blankets to keep me warm because by now I've gone cold with shock. By the time the ambulance had got to me I was fitting on and off, my heart didn't feel right at all but I was starting to have some sensation back in my right arm, just enough to know it was there. They wired me up to the ECG machine and began to look at my heart rhythm. I cannot remember what the results were but they said they wanted to bring me in. Because I lived one floor up in a flat they asked me if I could walk down the stairs. I couldn't believe it! but because I think of others before myself I didn't want to burden them with having to carry me, and because it is only down one flight of stairs I said I will walk it. I had made it down stairs and into the back of the ambulance and I started fitting once again. My partner's auntie had collected our son while all this was happening, and off to Brighton hospital we went. I remember being strapped to the bed with my body jolting and looking into my partner's eyes thinking, I'm a goner. I looked so deep into her remembering how much I loved her and wanting that memory of love to stay with me as I leave the physical world. We arrive at Brighton hospital and I'm now sitting in a wheelchair in line to be seen at the A&E department. I had now stopped fitting and was just shaking, I still didn't feel right at all, I knew something had changed, was it a stroke I wondered. A bed became free so I got in it and I laid down and then they began to wire me up to an ECG machine and asked me what had happened. I gave them all the details and they told me that I am to stay there for a while. I was having trouble talking because by now I am exhausted so I just laid back resting with the wires attached to me. After an hour or so they came back and checked the machine and told me that my heart is stable and I probably just had a panic attack and that I was now free to go home. I couldn't believe it, after all that had just happened and they put it down to a panic attack. I was lying relaxing in bed when it happened, I wasn't in panic, how dare they just chuck me back out on the street an hour later after all of that. So out of disgust I reluctantly left and went home. I didn't feel right after that and my heart beat was always beating to a different rhythm. I slowed right down after this as I had already thought I had had a stroke a while back while I was taking the methotrexate and that was down the left side of my body, and now I think I've just had one down the right side.

Time moves on and I've been indoors a lot now, just pottering about and watching films on Netflix, my stomach feels better as I'm no longer eating the methotrexate and despite all the pain I'm a lot happier as I've not had to deal with injecting myself anymore. I'm still taking my anti-depressant and a selection of pain killers.

During this time that I was stuck indoors taking it easy I had deeply been missing going out walking. I missed seeing the trees and watching and listening to the birds. I thought to myself that I have been stuck in for too long now, I really have to get out of here. Luckily my wheelchair arrived that week, it was all black and had big wheels at the back so I could control it myself. It looked really nice as wheelchairs go but what didn't look nice to me was the thought of me giving up my independence and having to ride in it. I stubbornly sat there for a whole week staring at it and thinking of all the people that would be laughing at me. I had always been a go faster type of person; if I did running it had to be for miles, if I rode my bike I had to be gone all day. I wasn't going to get in this wheelchair without a fight.

I went out with my partner a few times and took a walking stick leaving the wheelchair sitting there at home. I could handle the back pain that wasn't the cause that was stopping me from walking and I had worked from the age of sixteen with back pain every day. What was to be my problem though was these new pains that were in the sacro area. That pain was causing me loads of problems and was the main cause of all my walking difficulties. My partner kept saying we should have bought the wheelchair out with us, I knew she was right but I didn't want to give in so I stubbornly battled to keep going. The pain made my behaviour a challenge and before long I was always having to find somewhere to sit down while she would continue to look around the shop. I was realising that I was making us suffer every time we went out because I wouldn't use my wheelchair. So I started to stay home on my own and just refused to go out, that way I wouldn't affect my partner and my son's day by me being moody because of the pain that I was experiencing. Well after sitting at home for sometime looking at this wheelchair and crying on and off I finally caved in. One evening when our son was sleeping over at his nan's, I said to my partner can she take me out in my wheelchair, of course she said and she got up and started to get the wheelchair ready. I said hold on a minute not just yet, she asked why what's up and I said we will have to wait a bit longer until it becomes dark outside so that way nobody can see me and then we can go and give it a try, she agreed with a big grin upon her face. So we went out and in actual fact it was really lovely, I was so happy just to be able to breathe the fresh air and see the trees and listen to the birds while not struggling to physically walk. I decided that it's far better to be outside than not at all, so I began to use the wheelchair on a regular basis.

Chapter 4

Age thirty-three comes around. Happy birthday Russell.

This was to be a year of new beginnings.

Being out and about in the wheelchair wasn't too bad at all and before long everybody started to get used to seeing me in the wheelchair. My son would be sitting on my lap and my partner pushing us both along. Although I had picked a self-propelled wheelchair I hadn't realised just how hard it was to propel yourself along. In a supermarket it was fantastic as the floor is perfectly flat, not a single bump anywhere, but once you get outside it's a completely different story altogether. The slightest incline was extremely hard and if the ground sloped to one side it was a total nightmare. To self-propel was very hard indeed and it would always hurt my lower back where I had the Ankylosing Spondylitis. Before long though I would be in pain just from sitting in the wheelchair. I started to develop more widespread pains, I had pain in my elbows, in my hands, in my neck and my lower back and all I was doing was sitting in the wheelchair being pushed along. I had pains everywhere, even my veins were now beginning to hurt. My partner was now having to push me everywhere, even around the supermarket on their flat ground. We lasted sometime like this but eventually my outings were to get less and less. The pain had now spread throughout my entire body, I felt drained and uncomfortable. The stairs leading up to my flat were becoming impossible to handle even though it was just one flight, it was now too much. I started to stay at home a lot of the time again and I just told my partner to take our son out as it wasn't fair on both of them being stuck indoors with me. I was still juggling painkillers and by now I felt like I had eaten most of the periodic table. Some pills would make me sleep some would hype me up and by now I was starting to lose count of what I was actually putting into my system. I didn't feel like anything was working and my pain was so wide spread by now that I was struggling to function around the home. I was having accidents in the kitchen, in the bedroom, in the lounge and burning myself with hot water in the bathroom. I remember making a cup of tea and as I stood there while the kettle was boiling, I suddenly had no control over any of my movements and with a blank mind my hand decides to press itself against the outside of the boiling hot kettle. Afterwards I poured the boiling water into my cup and bobbed the tea bag around a bit, stirred the tea and then placed the hot spoon on the back of my hand. For some reason I didn't have any control over my bodily movements at all. I was running baths and not knowing how hot they were and just getting in and nearly passing out. My partner was going to have to monitor me, she would now run my baths and help me to get in and then wash me. She would make my breakfast, lunch and dinner and all my hot drinks. This went on for a while and eventually my hands and body were hurting so much my partner was having to feed me a couple of times a week. We decided we needed to move to an adapted home so we put things in motion straight away.

The council had found us a new home; it was on the ground floor and had a ramp access for the wheelchair and a wet room. We went to take a look at it and accepted it straight away. It's in a different town where neither myself or my partner have ever lived before and seen as I knew everybody in the town I was already in, I thought it would be a good start for us where nobody knows me so they can't remind me how active I used to be. It would be easier for my partner as she wouldn't have to help me as much. So the only problem I had was how am I going to pack all this stuff up and move us to another town while I'm ill. Luckily we got some help with the move. So over a few days me and my partner packed all our belongings up and prepared to move. We hired a van and that was that.

On the day of the move I strapped my back up and our friends placed all our belongings into the van for us and I drove us to our new home. Our friends took everything out of the van for us so all we had to do was unpack. We had made it, finally our life was going to be a bit easier and we can regularly all go out again as there were no more stairs. Or so we thought. I still had loads of pain all over my body from head to toe and we started to fill our home with a few bits to help, like a chair in the shower and a frame around the toilet, and a stool for in the kitchen. I was moving around in my wheelchair from room to room and wasn't really doing much anymore. I was still on pain medication and my anti-depressant. I was beginning to struggle with sitting upright in a chair again so I was lying down for periods at a time to recover. This pattern of lying down began to get longer and longer and I felt worse and worse. I was struggling to get out of bed to even use the toilet and ended up staying in for months. My skin had turned yellow and my tongue had something growing on the surface of it which didn't look great. All my skin was baggy and I had started to have full body fits again. So much for the great start I thought. We called the doctors out and here I am laid in bed unable to lift my arms and head and they are standing at the end of my bed confused as to why I'm so ill. They really had no explanation, nobody knew why I was fitting or why my skin was yellow. They suggested more tablets and they left. I was really beginning to lose myself again as I was very scared because nobody had any answers in how I could get better. I started to read the side effects of my anti-depressant tablets and I became convinced that it had to be that. Inside the side effects leaflet there was information about ectopic heartbeat, fitting, sweating, yellowing of skin etc. So while I laid there in bed I took to Google to try and find answers in order to get myself well. I felt I had been failed by the hospital and doctors. I had another episode, this time my heart beat went all crazy again, it stopped for a long pause and then three quick beats and then a big pause and then three quick beats, this happened three times and then it was normal for a few beats before it would do it again, every time it stopped I had this dull pain in my heart and I was holding my chest. I told my partner to call the ambulance. They came out and connected me up to the ECG machine and it showed I was having an ectopic heartbeat. I said that I think this is due to my anti-depressant and I showed them the leaflet that came with the medication and I pointed out to them the section that was to do with irregular heartbeats. They looked at it and said no it won't be that and asked if I have taken today's dose, I told them that I hadn't as I wasn't feeling well. They told my partner to get the tablet and give it to me whilst they were with me. Now by this time my heart was stopping and then doing quick beats and then stopping again, this happened two times and they said if it happens more than two times then I was to contact them again. I said it was happening three times and that's why I had called. They didn't seem worried and they printed out my ECG result and left. I was outraged and drained, I felt completely let down, yet again.

I made the decision to stop the anti-depressant tablet the very next day. I needed answers on how to get better and because the doctors couldn't help I had to come up with a new plan. Now as I previously said I had decided to stop taking the anti-depressant tablet and now I was going to have to be more extreme. I told my partner that I'm on so much medication that I have no idea which one could be causing me problems as all of them have side effects. I thought that it could even be the fact that I smoke cigarettes that could be doing this to me. By now I had grown increasingly desperate so I decided that I was going to stop all of my medication, that's it no more, not a single tablet. Only then will I know where I am and then, if I needed to I could then put one back in at a time and monitor its changes and effects. Most people including my partner would have thought this was a bad move as I was in so much pain and very ill. I remember thinking, what's the use in taking painkillers if they do not kill the pain? So I stopped all medication and began to fight the pain alone. During this physical detox I was to become more unwell but I had decided that no matter what, I'm not giving in. The pain became worse and worse, I had trouble eating, sleeping and just moving about the bed. My partner would set me up for the day, by making me lunch in advance and preparing drinks, ensuring that I could last on my own for a few hours so she could go out. As I laid there in so much pain I was having to close my eyes on and off as a coping mechanism to deal with the pain moving through my veins and every fibre of my being. I was exhausted and upset that I was missing out on life; I would watch the seasons change from the window next to my bed as I laid there regularly watching everything that Netflix had to offer. In a moment of extreme pain internally and externally I began to feel like I was dying. I started to become very worried as I was alone. I felt a big weight pushing down on me so strong that I was having trouble breathing and within a flash, I was found. I was lying on my back with my arms down by my sides and my spirit left my physical body. It was only very brief and while in the past I had experienced lucid dreaming and astral projection and many drug fuelled trips I knew that this was different. I had just died! I knew this because the feeling was completely different from the other experiences that I have had. This time I was met by my dead grandfather and my dead great-grandmother who is my grandfather's mother. They were standing beside my physical body. They were both standing the same side of me, my grandfather was nearest to me as he was standing alongside my chest area and my great-grandmother was standing in line with my knees. As my spirit left my physical body my grandfather and great-grandmother caught my spirit as it rose up out of my body and then my grandad looked at at his mum and said. One, two, three and they then both pushed down at the exact same time and pushed my spirit back into my physical body. Then they were gone and I felt that spiritually I was now in a different place. My physical body was still laying there in the bed but my spirit was someplace else and I was aware of this. It was like when you remotely view a situation in your psyche without having to physically be there. Next thing standing over me were three extra-terrestrials, I couldn't move or speak. I felt like I was laid on an operating table in a different dimension, I was feeling very relaxed as I wasn't experiencing any pain at all. They scanned my physical body by sight and were viewing all my internal organs, and then they stopped at my chest area and communicated to each other. They then reached in and removed my heart and then placed a golden heart back in its place. They scanned my body again and then the room was empty. I knew that I had been somewhere but wasn't sure if what happened was real or not. It felt very real and I could see and hear them as it was all happening. I laid there crying because in the past when I've experienced astral projection or drug trips I've always been the driver, the one that's in control, so even though I was questioning what had just happened I knew in my heart that really this experience was real. This did just happen. They had found me when I was completely lost. So at the age of thirty three I had died and ascended and instantly had learned more about life than we know it. It turns out that this was the age that Jesus first died. Everything was different from that point on and everything instinctively felt different too. I felt relieved to know that I wasn't alone and that our loved ones are always there for us. I felt positive about everything for the first time in a long time. I continued to stay off the medication and fight the pain myself.

Chapter 5

Thirty-four comes around. Happy birthday Russell.

This was to be a challenging year full of spiritual connection.

Now, there were lots going on as my senses had become extremely sensitive after the ascension. I couldn't handle sounds whether it was the phone ringing, the television playing or people talking. I started to wear ear plugs for the best part of the day. While I was aware that I had been visited I wasn't aware of the ongoing changes I was to experience, this was a new type of sensitivity. I was still in a lot of widespread pain but I was mobile, I would still lie down for periods at a time in bed but i wasn't completely stuck there. I wasn't happy with my muscle wastage though and was now wondering if I could exercise to get some muscle back. So I started attempting to do more; at first I was just up for longer and trying to help around the house. I was experiencing vision problems again, except this time it was as though a beam of light was projecting from the front of my face, around the forehead area. I was finding standing up awkward as it felt strange at first, it was as though I was having to learn how to walk again. I was a bit clumsy and I was having to sit down for breaks as my heart would start to tell me that it wasn't happy. I knew one thing though; I wasn't going to give up, ever. This became a daily thing, I would try to wash up each day, just for something to achieve and to keep me moving. So there I was ear plugs in and doing the washing up. My partner was walking in and out of the kitchen, now I know I couldn't hear her but as she was walking in and out I felt as though her movements were affecting my own heart rhythm. So now I was thinking that I need to double check this, so I didn't say anything to her I just carried on washing up and waited for her to next come in and see what my heart feels like. Sure enough in she walked and my heart felt strange again. I've sat down to recover and waited a few minutes and then carried on washing up. I didn't tell my partner as I didn't want her to worry I thought I would just keep an eye on it myself.

The next day my partner went out so without telling her I tried exercising. By now I had done a few days at washing up so I thought I would give it ago. I didn't do anything too crazy and just worked out at home. I used to do martial arts so I thought if I did some light bag work then my body might respond as it's an exercise that I used to do, a lot. How wrong was I. I must have lasted about four minutes and boom something felt very wrong with my body. I had never had this feeling before and I wasn't out of breath. I was tingling all over and I felt like my heart was going to stop, so I laid straight down on the floor in a coffin shape waiting for it to pass. After about twenty minutes of panic that I was going to have a heart attack or stroke I finally got back up off the floor. It was to be sometime before I would attempt this exercise again.

I was also having problems psychologically, I kept seeing different faces. Now these weren't just faces floating about my home that everybody could see, these seemed like mind intrusions. It was as though every time I blinked I was seeing a face, whether it was my nan's face or my mum's or a complete stranger. These faces appeared so close that it was making me feel uncomfortable. Sometimes I felt like I was looking out of their eyes and I could see them moving around in their homes. My hearing was still very sensitive and I was experiencing anxiety whenever my phone would ring, I wasn't ready to talk to anyone over the phone. I was switching plug sockets off when I wasn't wearing ear plugs, as I could hear the electricity buzzing through the walls. My senses were so strong it was as though all I could see were heat waves inside my home.

My partner was out feeding the ducks with our son at our local pond and my mobile phone started ringing. The caller id said it was my mum. Now I hadn't seen my mum for years and knew that I needed to answer this call. I started to go into panic and put a pillow over the phone and started to pace about my home. I was struggling to breath and I was now hiding from my phone and awaiting my partner to come home and sort this matter out for me. By the time my partner gets home I'm a mess and full of questions, what do you think it's about I asked? She told me to not worry about it and go and lay down in bed as I was in physical pain. I left my phone with my partner and went to lie down. Later that evening I woke up to hear my phone ringing in the living room where my partner was sitting. I could hear my partner talking to my brother, he had come over from Australia so I knew something was up and started to have another panic attack. After a lot of noise my partner comes into the bedroom and tells me that my brother wanted me to go to Brighton hospital immediately as my stepdad was in intensive care. My partner had said that I was asleep because she knew I was going to need time to settle before I could go. The next day I decided that I would go, I hadn't seen my stepdad for years and I arrived at the hospital in my wheelchair. I received the news from my mum that he had just had surgery. During the time I didn't see them he had been diagnosed with cancer of the stomach and oesophagus. When I arrived he was in intensive care recovering from the operation. It was an emotional first meeting and afterwards I started to regularly see my mum and stepdad again. I also started to see my nana again and began to slowly reintegrate myself back into the family.

I was still having problems with my environment and I kept feeling like high amounts of electricity was moving through my body and I kept sensing the presence of people around my home. These people were in fact spirits. My son and partner's energy was also effecting me a lot. All of this was making it a challenge to see my family but I was going for short visits. When I was visiting them at their homes I was seeing if I could feel the presence of any spirits. Sure enough I could feel something. Something changed once I had been to my nana's old home, I returned back to my home and everything started to change. I became very cold and then hot and very cold again and then hot. This kept happening and I had no idea what was going on, so I decided to go and take a shower so my temperature would behave itself. As I walked up my hall way I saw something, I saw a black dog's tail and the dog had gone into my bedroom. Now I don't own a dog and I instinctively knew straight away that it was my old dog Black Max. Black Max had been my best friend in my early childhood and was no longer alive. I had seen his spirit and I felt ecstatic. I rushed to tell my partner what I had seen and then I got into the shower. While in the shower

I started to think back to when I was younger and I thought that I used to see spirits, I was a bit confused about it all but kept an open mind.

I was due a hospital appointment with the specialist and I was getting worried as to what I might see. I was starting to get worried everywhere I went as I was thinking, when will the spirits next show themselves. About five days before the date of the appointment I was seeing something in my mind's eye, it was money. I could see a fat roll of money with a rubber band wrapped around it. This image wouldn't leave me no matter how hard I tried to forget it. On the day of my appointment the weather wasn't that great, it was windy and raining. So we put on our coats and started to make our way there. This image was still in my mind's eye all this time and I said to my partner I wonder if it will ever go? My partner was unsure as she had never experienced any of these things herself. So we got off the bus and started to slowly walk towards the hospital, as we got near we had one road left to cross. We stood there being blown about and rained on and when the traffic became clear we crossed, just before we made it to the other side I saw in front of me a wet five pound note stuck to the kerb.

I reached down in amazement and picked it up. I couldn't believe it, how did a note stay there in these weather conditions I said to my partner. I wondered if this was to be the money I was seeing in my mind's eye, I know it wasn't a roll but it was still a note, sure enough within an hour the image that was in my mind's eye disappeared. I realised then that not only could I see spirits but I could also be guided by them too.

As the weeks went on my life started to get stranger still. My general health was changing and I started to go out to car boot fairs with my partner and her family, I was using the wheelchair but was attempting to walk around some of it. As I was walking round I came across a picture, it was a sketch of an owl, my mum's favourite. It was drawn in black and white and was housed within a tatty frame, the owl had been given a name too, he was Fred. I said to my partner my mum would like that, she said did I want to get it and I said no as we didn't have much money. As I walked away all I could see in my mind's eye was this picture and I was getting a feeling that my dead grandad was urging me to buy it for my mum. As I tried to ignore this feeling I continued to walk around, the visualisation of this owl picture in my mind's eye was getting stronger to which point I told my partner that I must go back and get it. So back I went and I bought it. Now as I said before that the frame it was in wasn't in great shape, it had damage to it but the picture was fine. So I took it to the framers upon where I decided I wanted a template window to fit the picture and I wanted the picture to be housed in a wooden frame. I had chills as I dropped the picture off and was feeling overcome with emotion. I now knew that these were signs that my grandad was with me at that time. I left the picture there and was due to collect it within a week or so. Due to the fact that I had been so overcome with emotion and sensations I had been having whilst in the framers and over the past few days, I had planned to stay indoors and recover for a few days.

After two days of staying at home I decided to take my partner and son to the park in Saltdean. For some reason I kept feeling an inner pull that was drawing me to the town where my grandad and Doris used to live. Because my nana still lives there in the same house that my grandad built we decided to park the car at hers and walk down as it was only a short distance from the park. Once at the park my partner is playing with our son and I had a moment to myself. I decided to talk to my grandad out loud but quietly enough that my partner couldn't hear me. I said, gramps if this is all real then please can you give me a sign right now. Sure enough I begin to hear an engine in the distance, this engine sounded like a plane. I kid you not the skies were completely clear and out of nowhere along came a spitfire plane right in front of me! A spitfire! The reason for my shock was because my grandad used to fly a spitfire plane for many years in the RAF. I was blown away and started to believe that this was all in fact very real indeed.

The picture hadn't been completed on the date that I had been given and somehow I knew there was a reason behind this. On the day that I went to pick up the picture yet again I had a feeling that I wasn't alone. The picture looked perfect inside the new frame and I noted down its collection date. I contacted my mum and told her that I have a picture for her and two days later I went over and delivered her the picture, luckily she liked it, well done gramps.

I decided to go visit my nana as I wanted to tell her all about my news and to see if I could see spirits in her home. I knew that the collection date from the framers was an important date to her so I also wanted to see if I was right. I showed my nana the picture of my mum's owl picture and said that it was chosen by my grandad, her husband. She didn't look too convinced so I decided to challenge her with the collection date and boom. I was right that this date was an important date; it was her wedding anniversary which was due in one month's time. I thought bingo, that's what my grandad was trying to tell me. So I told my nana that grandad is still around and he has been guiding me. I told her that he's aware that your wedding anniversary is near and he wants to tell you that he loves you very much and that he is still here. She got up and went into the lounge and returned to give me an old game that we used to play together, Chinese Chequers. She said I could take it home and keep it as her hands were too bad with arthritis to play it now. I began to tell nana about my other experiences that I had been having too. I told her about grandad and his mum pushing me back inside my body and how it's all been different from that point. I said that I had found money outside the hospital and that I had seen Black Max. She started to tell me stories about Black max and how much we loved each other, he was my best friend and followed me everywhere. She told me that Max had eaten the wooden top off her pepper pot once, so only the matching salt pot was out on the kitchen side. She said it was a shame as she really missed not having the set anymore. I remember leaving nanas that day in full belief that my gift was working so I decided to try and communicate back to my grandad through meditation. I had said to my grandad that if you would like to give a present to nana then just guide me to what it is and I will get it for you. A few days later I started to think about the pepper pot and how the salt and pepper used to be an old wedding gift to symbolise bride and groom. I decided that I would replace the pepper pot, so the hunt began. Because the pots were old I had to track it down on the internet, surely enough I had found a set and I bought them. My nana used to have a piano in the front room too and the card that I picked out had music notes with two birds on it and it read "love makes the heart sing". I wrapped it all up and put everything inside a box. I turned up on her anniversary day and gave her the box and a kiss, I said I can't stop but this is for you to open at your leisure. The next time I saw her she said thank you for the gift and card and asked why the salt and pepper, I said it symbolises bride and groom, so you are now complete again.

Back home I was very aware of movement within my home and I kept having these hot and cold sensations. Every time I was around my partner I kept having a sensation in my heart again, it was as though somebody was squeezing it. So as usual I went and had a shower to try and stop these hot and cold sensations. As I walked back into my lounge I saw a lady sat on my sofa. This lady wasn't in her physical body and was presented to me in a black and white image. She was wearing a dress that had daisy flowers on it. She made me know that the dress was the colour blue. I froze and said to my partner that somebody is sitting next to you on the sofa. I described what I was seeing to my partner and she wasn't sure who that could be. So I sat down on the other end of the sofa and we tried to think who this lady might be. Just sitting next to my partner was making my heart feel strange again and I decided to get up and go to the toilet. When I was at the toilet I was spoken to in my right ear this lady's voice said, tell her I passed from the heart. So I called out to my partner and said, this lady that has that dress with the daisies on it, just told me to tell you that she passed from the heart. Straight away my partner said it was her great nana Emily and that her favourite flowers were daisies and yes she used to wear a dress with them on. Wow I thought, this was incredible as this was the first time that it wasn't my family but it was hers. I went and sat back in the lounge and started to watch television. Next thing I knew was I felt a shadow standing over me. Now this shadow was different from any other that I had ever experienced as this shadow contained a body mass. I could feel the person inside the shadow, I became worried and said to my partner how do you fight off a shadow. Within my mind's eye I was starting to see a picture of a man with a large trophy cabinet which was full of trophies. I said to my partner that it's a man, he's showing me his trophies and really boasting about how great he is at his sport. I couldn't tell what he had won the trophies for but he was persistent in letting me know that he was the best. I said the man is very tall and is now showing me that he is standing behind somebody awaiting his turn. The next thing was he darted across my lounge in front of the television and in doing so made my television click, he then ran back across to where I was and made the television click again as he went past. My partner was trying hard to think as to who this man might be, so we phoned my partner's auntie who lives with her mum and dad and told her about great nan Emily and that now this man is standing here showing me trophies. She said it was great grandad Albert and that he used to play darts and won lots of trophies for it. She said she would get the old photos out that her mum had got so she could show us the next time we were over. We go over to their house the very next day and I got shown some pictures and there within these photos was the image I had been shown, great grandad with all his darts trophies and great nan in her dress with daisies on it. That day while at their house I saw two more spirits. I saw a lady sitting in an armchair, this armchair wasn't part of the suite yet somehow, she had her own chair. This was all getting too much for me by this point so I went out into the back garden to calm down and then saw a man standing at their back door smoking. I didn't know what to do and so

I pushed passed and went back into the lounge. These spirits decided to keep opening and closing the lounge door to which everybody was starting to wonder what was going on. Then as my partner's nan went to retreat into the kitchen then great nan Emily touched her hand which made a spark noise and nan shot up in the air. I didn't say anything at that time but everybody was on high alert, so I said to my partner we had better leave so we went home.

Over the next few days I started to wonder how do you protect yourself from all of this or can you not turn it off. My friend came over to see if I was alright as I'd told her all about what had been happening. We sat down just talking on the sofa and then the next thing I see was a blue budgie fly around her head and into a cage on a stand. Somehow I knew that this was a bird she had when she was younger. I thought well I'm going to have to tell her and let's just hope I'm not wrong as don't want to look silly. So I told her and it turned out that I was right. She did have a blue budgie when she was younger and it was kept in a cage on a stand. Her mother told her that she was very upset when the blue budgie died. I had guessed that when the bird died it left behind an emotional mark on her heart that needed healing and this is why I could see the bird.

A few weeks later I was having problems with energy again, I was noticing that if my son had a paddy or if my partner was stressed it would change the things that I would see in my mind's eye and would affect my mood and energy levels. One particular evening my son had been playing up and my partner was arguing with him, this changed the energy in my home and I then felt like I was being attacked inside my mind's eye. It was as though all the energy I was receiving was negative and I found this really unbearable and I didn't know how to stop it. I decided to try and go to bed early in the hope it would stop. Well it didn't stop and I was seeing horrible things over and over. I decided to switch the television on in the bedroom and try to watch a film to see if it would stop, it didn't. Later on everybody was now asleep and by one am I had grown desperate. I got out of bed and went into the lounge, this didn't help either as the room was bigger than my bedroom and I felt like I was stuck inside a horror film. Doris appeared in my mind's eye. Now Doris used to live across the road from my nana and I used to go over to see her when I was much younger. She was no longer here in the physical world. So she appeared in my mind's eye and gave me instructions. She told me to go into my bedroom and get the Chinese Chequers box that my nana had given to me and to take it into the lounge so I went and got the box and took the box into the lounge. I had a coffee table in the middle of the lounge and she told me to place the box on the table, so I did. The room was filled with static energy as I could see it all but when I placed this box down on the table it was like magic, all the energy within the room lowered and cleared. It was absolutely amazing. Doris instructed me to regularly burn sage and place candles around my home. I have burned sage and placed candles every day since this experience, and I have found that it clears the harsh energy out of my home. My nana has since told me that Doris was a healer and a medium here in the physical world; I now regularly follow Doris's instructions as I travel along my spiritual path.

I started to regularly meditate as I found that it was helping with the physical pain and was helping me psychologically too. During my meditations I kept on being shown the three main pyramids in

Egypt they kept stressing the importance of these pyramids and their alignment with the stars. Then they showed me the milky way and said that if I was to find where the extra-terrestrials that changed my heart came from, then we were to travel through the centre of it. I was led to believe that a black hole was a gateway into another dimension, their dimension. Next I was taken by a guide who appeared as a tribesman holding a long spear and wearing a leather cloth. He took me to the top of a hill and pointed to the birds, to the buffalo and across the land and told me that I was connected to all of this and in previous lives I had been everything. I was shown how to ground my energy to mother earth and then I was also shown the importance of the Sun and the Moon and how they correspond to our physical bodies, the Moon dominates the left side of our body while the Sun dominates our right side, I was told to bring both into duality in order to connect. Sometimes I pictured myself flying from place to place. I would fly over my mum's house and check in on her and I would regularly fly to nana's house and would picture me checking in on nana. I began to start seeing my great nan in these meditations and I would dance with her inside my nana's house. During these moments I would feel a presence in my room and all around me. My body would always tingle during these moments. As my eyes were closed during these meditations I couldn't physically see a spirit in my room but because in my mind's eye I was dancing with my great nan I assumed that it was her in the room with me. How amazing I thought, she was there standing next to me while I meditated. I was moved to tears as I could feel her touching me.

I decided by now that there had been too many things going on and that I need to now know what I was. Myself and my partner started looking for somebody to help. We asked nana as she had previously said about Doris, but my nana didn't know of anybody. We asked my mum but she also didn't know who could help. I was in need of answers and for the first time ever I decided I was going to have to see a medium. We had found a lady that was based in Brighton who wasn't too far from us and we booked to see her. That day she was on East Street doing readings. I was so nervous, what if I've had a psychotic episode I thought, what happens if I'm crazy. I had to put all my fears to one side and I went and sat down with this lady. She said let's have a look at you then, and I instantly felt like Neo when he saw the oracle in the Matrix film. She looked at me and within seconds knew what I was. I finally received my label. Divine Light Psychic; natural gift from God with the ability to talk directly to God and the angels, she said that I could do everything and that I had all the gifts. She said to me, you see things, don't you? I didn't say much, but she wasn't giving up on me and asked me to read her right there and then. I said that I had never done a reading outside before but she prompted me to read her. So I looked down at the ground and I saw a white rabbit on a square patch of grass above her head. I told her and she started crying. I thought she was winding me up at first and I laughed, she moved the hair further away from her eyes and looked deep into me saying, I loved that rabbit and it was attacked in its hutch overnight. I remember thinking oh no this is a great start I have just made her cry. She told me to carry on and the next thing I saw was a lady ringing an old school bell and then she placed the bell on the table in front of me. This turned out to be the lady's old dinner lady that she had grown fond of when she was at school and she confirmed that she was on the other side. I was then able to remotely view the inside of her home and found myself in one of the bedrooms. I felt drawn to a fish tank that turns out that it was kept in her loft and she was recently thinking about bringing it down to use again. I was told to go home and start putting out business cards, and begin work as a medium, but I didn't. I was now questioning it all again wondering if it was all just a fluke and that if I had a customer would I see anything. I decided to leave it and just see if I get more readings off anybody that I came into contact with.

I remember sitting up in bed one morning after this unpleasant vision. During my sleep I was shown a family photo within a silver edged frame. There were three people in the picture, a man then a child then a lady, within my dream this man took out a black pen and crossed himself out of the picture. The energy that I was given with this vision was that the man was going to end his life. As I sat there in bed I remember thinking, if only I knew where this man was then maybe I could help him to not go through with it. I sat there thinking and waiting for my partner to wake up and told her what I had seen and felt. I didn't get shown where the man lived and the image wasn't in enough detail for me to know what he looked like or when it was going to happen or if it had already happened. The next day was when one of my neighbours was leaving her home I said good morning, how are you today. She replied, not too good as my cousin has taken his life, leaving behind his beautiful children. She was very sad and I had completely forgotten about my dream the morning before so I didn't put two and two together. I said to her, I've been able to communicate with spirits a lot recently so if I hear anything I will let you know, and left it at that. I went back inside my home and told my partner and she said straight away, what if the dream you had was of that person. I suddenly remembered and thought oh my god she must be right. When I awoke the next morning my partner and our son were still asleep, so I got up out of bed without waking them and went to sit in the window of my lounge. I decided to put my headphones on and listen to music. As I did this I shut my eyes and what I was about to be shown was unbelievable. I felt the chills and was pulled into a vision, I found myself sitting in the driver's seat at the top of a cliff in a small car with a distressed man in the passenger seat looking at photos and crying. He was unable to calm down and was punching the dashboard. His psyche was battling with life and death. The stresses within his life were making him want to end it all but the thought of his children was keeping him here. As I sat there watching unable to help I could feel all his emotions. After a few minutes we swapped seats. As he moved into the driver's seat I'm automatically moved into the passenger seat. By this point I remember that I'm trying to feed him positive thoughts to keep him alive but he wasn't aware of me. He then starts the car engine and drives hitting the kerb before he takes us over the edge of the cliff. I could see and feel all of this and then bang the car hits the ground and bursts into flames. This vision now stops in my mind's eye and this man then gave me the information of the date that it happened, and his name and that he was the man that crossed himself out of that picture from my previous dream. It was very sad as I felt this was my neighbour's cousin. Now I realised why I couldn't help him, because his death had already happened. I wrote everything down and went to sit with her to give her the news. She confirmed that this was in fact her cousin. Later that day I was at a shop and I happened to see the front page of the newspaper and there it was, the scene that I had been shown. My details were correct, and I was amazed. I remember thinking and saying to my partner, I wish I was in control of it rather than it being in control of me.

Later that week I was meditating as normal and something happened. I was dancing in the lounge with great nan again but this time during the dance she stopped. Now there were never any doors when we would dance, I would just appear in my mind to be in my nanas lounge and there would be great nan and then I would just arrive back home. This time after she stopped the dance she pointed to her right and there was a long dark hall way with a light on at the end. The end room was in the direction of the front room. I looked back at her and she stomped her foot and pointed in the same direction again. So I turned and as I took one step I had made it to the end of the hallway. I stepped inside the room and looked left as to where my grandad used to sit and sitting in the chair was my grandad. I felt overcome with emotion and he said, come and sit down son. He said to me I know how bad your life has been but it will all get better from here on out. I kept my eyes closed studying his face for a few minutes and then opened my eyes again. I began looking on the internet for help and saw a lady called Heidi Sawyer I knew this had to be a sign because my grandad's name was John Arthur Sawyers.

I emailed Heidi for help straight away. I was desperate for answer as to why all these things have been happening to me lately. I really needed to know how to control it so my life wouldn't be invaded at inappropriate times. Heidi Sawyer is an intuition expert, a writer and also a teacher at Hay House. She replied back to my email with great understanding of my situation. For the first time in my life I actually found somebody who was like me. She knew me even without meeting me, she didn't need to know me for years and yet she got me. Straight away she begins to help me and puts me in touch with her team and I have been looked after and have felt safe ever since. I decided to buy Heidi's book, Highly Intuitive People. As I sat there reading it she started to remind me bits of my life that I had forgotten about. I could relate most of my life to hers and I was finally relieved to know that I wasn't the only one of my kind. I decided to take online courses with her and straight away she knew what was going on. She said to me, now let's stop that light from beaming out of the front of your head, we can't have you walking around like that. I thought, how does she know this? I've not told her that this is happening. Sure enough she directed the light to beam inside. She told me she knew about my swollen big toe that I've had from the age of twelve. This toe had been the biggest annoyance of my entire life and yes Heidi Sawyer knew about it and how to make it better! What an angel.

Chapter 6

Thirty-five comes round. Happy Birthday Russell.

This was to be a clean-up of my inner world.

I had to quit smoking and changed a few things in my life. Quitting smoking was a hard one to achieve, but I remained positive as I had quit before. I started by trying to reduce the amount that I smoked as really I wasn't ready to let go just yet. This went on for about two weeks and I wasn't winning. It had to go and this time I had to stay quit forever. I looked in the shops at all the nicotine replacement products. Would it be the gum or the inhalator, or a patch, or mints, all these options to choose from. I started reading the packets to see what strength I would need. This is where I had a problem as all the products were going to give me more nicotine than I was now already smoking. Oh dear I thought, now what am I going to do? I asked in the shop if there we any options of lower amounts of nicotine and they said that there wasn't. I had no options left I would have to go cold turkey. I returned home and threw all of my smoking things away, all the lighters, all the ashtrays, all the rizlas, that was it everything. Cleaned the house so it was smoke free and washed all my clothes then the battle began. Now when you quit smoking the first thing you notice is the time, how slowly it moves and as it moves slowly you would remind yourself that at this time you would have been smoking. The other thing you think of is I can't enjoy a cup of tea without a smoke. You eat some food and normally you would wash it all down with a smoke. If I was ever angry I would smoke. So you now realise that somehow you need to fill all these gaps. Not easy as habits are either for reward, relaxing, or suppression. I decided that I would have to sleep through it, so when the cravings would rob me of my sanity I would go to sleep. This technique actually works. However you cannot sleep all the time so you are still going to need willpower. In the end I broke the cycle and I am now smoke free. What was next? Alcohol, no more getting drunk, this was a battle as when you go food shopping the alcohol is always in the middle of the store. They also situate alcohol promotions on the ends of the aisles so every corner you turn, boom it's there looking at you. Like the smoking though I hung on in there and beat the beast. Caffeine was next it had to go to. No more flying with red bull, it was now time to land. My old friend sugar had to be reduced too, my highest intake of sugar was through chocolate and now that I wasn't smoking I had been reaching for the chocolate when I was angry in order to suppress the emotion. Oh boy this wasn't fair and I stomped my feet a few times, however it needed to be done. I had to retrain my brain that when I was feeling angry I couldn't smoke, I couldn't eat chocolate I just had to deal with it. I achieved this through meditation; if anger came up I would go sit in a quiet room and meditate until it had gone. After a few months of this I can now say that I'm a lot less angry now. I have a deeper sense of calm and solitude and am much happier for it. I now regularly meditate and it's been very beneficial to my physical and spiritual health. I control my pain though meditation and am not on any medication.

I was noticing spiritual movement within my home but hadn't received any communication. I continued with my meditations and my regular burning of sage and lighting candles and was due to finish my final course. I began to ask my spirit guides for signs as to when to take the leap and advertise myself as a Medium. One evening my grandad just let me know that he was there with me, it was only a little nudge. When he was very sick during his last days he always kept a bag of dolly mixtures beside his bed and used to let us have a few when I was child. During this evening the thought of dolly mixtures arrived in my mind followed by his presence to which I found very comforting. As you know my grandad also flew a spitfire plane during his time in the RAF and now on a daily basis he has been flying planes over my head whenever I feel in doubt about my current path. Even if I'm indoors he will make sure that the plane is so loud that I wouldn't be able to not hear it passing by. So it would seem that all the signs of encouragement and guidance from my spirit guides are there and yet here I am still wondering when to make the jump.

During my sleep I received a full reading. I am always aware of what is a dream and what is a message or a premonition so straight away I could tell that this wasn't a dream. The vision involved a young girl at a get together with three of her friends. She showed me that she was laughing with her friends and felt carefree and happy. They were experimenting with drugs and the drug that I picked up on was ecstasy. She had taken one of the tablets and was having a good time with her friends. During this time I saw her friends start to worry about her as they thought something wasn't right, they told her that her face didn't look right. She shrugged it off in disbelief and tried to continue to enjoy herself, she felt fine albeit she felt a lot of pressure around the head area. After a few minutes the worry that her friends had expressed to her started to make it difficult for her to fully let go and relax back into that carefree moment she was previously experiencing. She decided to go inside and look in the mirror. Once she started looking into the mirror she was first drawn to checking her pupil size, they were very wide and hypnotic and then she started to study her face, her face seemed distorted and she could start to see that something wasn't right, she thought that she was going to die and began to get scared. Her heart began to beat quicker as she realised that her friends had been telling her that truth after all. Panic set in and she ran out of the bathroom to rejoin her friends. She was screaming for them to call her an ambulance, they were all panicking as she was quickly looking worse. As they were waiting for the ambulance she knew that it was too late and she was going to die. Upon arrival to the hospital they learned that unfortunately it was too late and there wasn't anything that they could do, she said goodbye to her family and friends and after a few hours she had passed away. Tragically I was to see this on social media twenty four hours later.

I decided that I should take steps towards working as a medium and decided to make up a business card. So I sat down with my partner and opened the laptop and started to make up a card, after making the card I still didn't press the button to finalise my order. I was still unsure as to when I should make the move into mediumship work, so yet again I asked for more signs. I had said to my partner that since the ascension I felt like I was slowly turning into a lighthouse and that my light was a beacon that would call all spirits towards me. My light would also shine healing light for everybody here in the physical word and they would be attracted to it and be drawn towards me. About two days after receiving that young girls news I woke up to check my Instagram page, as I do every morning as Doreen Virtue pulls an angel card for everybody. This particular morning the card she pulled represented career change and the picture on the card was a light house. Well what a good start to the day that was as sure enough this was indeed a sign to take the jump. Still I asked for more signs, just to be sure. That morning I was going to a car boot sale and I was on the hunt for signs to let me know whether the time was indeed now. So there I am walking around this car boot sale and the first thing that I saw was a little Swiss wooden chalet, when you lifted the roof up it played music. It brought back an instant memory of my childhood as I distinctly remember my mum having one on display at her home. I hadn't seen it for years as at some point she must have packed it away or sold it, could this in fact be her actual Swiss chalet. I decided to take a photograph which I would later send to my mum. A few aisles later and I saw an old vinyl album it was Michael Jackson's history album, I instantly had another flash back to my childhood as I used to own this album on cassette tape. I remember listening to it on my own in my bedroom and studying the album art in great detail as the front picture contained so much activity. I had always felt overwhelmed with emotion as I sat there listening to "heal the world", this track meant so much to me and I always thought that one day I would in fact heal our earth that we all share. I thought I would heal how people interacted with one another and put an end to all wars and starvation. No animal suffering, no children suffering, no earth suffering, just everything in balance all held together with love and respect. I had always felt a deep connection to everything and had always found it difficult watching all the chaos within the world and I was always amazed at how poorly adults treated each other. I must of been at an age that I was starting to take notice of the media and was still all innocent trying to understand the world that I was born into. I sat in isolation absorbing every emotion of the album for quite some time, I remember just staring at the bedroom light bulb for hours, and frantically doing mathematics. Little did I know that I was charging up my pineal gland and I was obviously being channelled into having a deep interest in numerology. I didn't buy the vinyl album and continued to walk around the boot fair. After two more aisles the signs were about to all land in one go. I arrive at a stall and I see this lady that's selling a few bits and she had brought her dog with her for a bit of company, this other lady that was walking passed started to talk to her as she had seen her at a previous boot sale. She was drawn to the dog and she said out loud "that dog is called Tilly isn't it?" To which the lady at the stall replied "yes it is, she's very old now bless her". Immediately I was taken back to my childhood again and this time was because our first family dog was called Tilly, I remember thinking here we go again. The next stall was full of odd bits and inside an open box was a few pictures in tatty frames, I noticed some words were in one of the picture frames and I decided to read it, it reads as follows;

Memories build a special bridge

Our memories build a special bridge

when loved ones have to part

To help us feel we're with them still

and soothe a grieving heart.

Our memories span

the years we shared,

preserving ties that bind,

They build a special bridge of love

and bring us peace of mind.

I saw this as a sign and decided to get it despite its tatty frame.

So I walked to the next stall and boom! laid on a blanket before my feet I see an angel book and next to it "The Lightworker's Way" by Doreen Virtue I couldn't believe it ! laid there on this blanket next to Doreen's book was "Gratitude A Way of Life" by Louise Hay ! and next to that was another angel book. Wow three stalls all next to each other and all these signs, I could of jumped up and down and screamed. I told the lady on the stall that I had been asking for signs about when I should start work as a medium and then I gave detail about all the signs leading up to these books. I didn't hesitate and I brought them straight away.

The very next day I was due to do more studies with Heidi Sawyer, I had been studying with her for some time now and the course that I was on at that time was called "The Lavender Club". Within the club there were modules which would be released in stages and also live sessions in which you would connect over video call on the internet and talk with Heidi while the other students would watch and listen. Upon this particular session at the club we were all asked to fill out a questionnaire to track our stages of development. I wasn't sure what stage I was at so I was very hesitant in sending my answers back, so late lunchtime Monday I sent mine off, just four hours before class. I was understood that if your questionnaire wasn't received early then you probably wouldn't be speaking live with Heidi, that was fine with me I thought. So the time arrived and the class had begun there were about a hundred plus people on line, Heidi was talking away and then said if anybody is willing to talk then just click the "raise hand" button on the screen, so I clicked the button thinking well I might as well as the chances of me being picked would be slim. There I am sitting there with my hair and face unshaven looking a complete mess and boom ! she says "let's go live to Russell right now!" Oh dear my heart nearly exploded and I went live. During this live session I told her what had happened yesterday at the car boot sale, that I had seen lots of signs and that I thought the signs meant that I was ready to start work as a medium. Well I was wrong as the signs had in fact meant that I had stuffed an issue down deep within my system that stemmed from my very early childhood. Oh dear I thought, this was going to be emotional. Heidi was going to release this block right there live in front of over a hundred people. I allowed myself to feel the emotion but I refused to let a single tear fall from my face, after the energy and emotions were released I was told that I had been ready to do readings for some time and why hadn't I already started. I voiced my concern that I was worried that spirit wouldn't show up as there are no guarantees and I really don't like letting people down. Heidi told me that I was to start doing readings now and that by the next course I had to show the class that I had actually done a paid reading. Heidi had received forty emails from students that evening wanting me to read them, a few weeks later a block of five emails from students arrived in my emails, this was to be the start of my readings.

I booked my first reading in and had a few days to wait until the appointment. I was plunged into panic and doubt after I had booked it, lots of thoughts going through my mind, how will I help? will I be any help? will I be right? what happens if I'm wrong? I was pacing around getting hot and cold. The first reading was to be done over Skype, I thought to myself how will this work as normally I am sitting in front of the person face to face, panic sets in.

During the few days wait before the reading I was lucky enough to be unknowingly tested by a friend. We were talking on the phone and she told me that she was thinking about taking on a new job in a garden centre, straight away I felt the energy increase throughout my body and then in my mind's eye I saw a little shop that she would own. I told her that although she would be happy working with plants I do not see her working at the garden centre. I could see her running her own little florist, the type of small shop that specialises in delivering that personal touch, that warm conversation and that welcoming smile. I could hear the brass bell chime as you opened the shop door, and furthermore she was loved and liked by everyone. Her speciality was dealing with the public in a personal way while delivering the very best flowers. Without realising it I had just given a reading over the phone. Later that evening I spoke to her partner and he reflected upon his day at work about how he was once again left in the balance as to whether or not he had acquired a permanent position in his new job. Once again the energy came over me and I felt compelled to tell him about what was coming up. He's a very skilful man and I am lucky enough to have seen his brilliant work. He can fit bathrooms and kitchens and much more, all to a very high specification. I could see that he would be more rewarded if he went it alone and used his skills by working for himself installing beautiful kitchens and bathrooms within people's homes. He is also a very kind and honest man so I felt the customers would also feel secure with having him carry out the work within their home. He had a previous bad experience trapped within his subconscious that was making him hold back, he talked about it and I told him don't let that block define you. After the chat I decided to go and ask a question to my angel cards for him. As I sat there asking the question "should he become self-employed" the card that jumped out and landed on the floor said "you are ready". Brilliant I thought! I phoned him straight back and gave him the news. So as luck would have it I had done two readings over the phone before my Skype appointment was due.

So the day of the reading arrives, my appointment was at twelve thirty over Skype. I got up and did all the normal things, shower breakfast and chakra balancing. I was conscious of the fact that I needed to not have a tummy full of food but also to not be hungry so I had my breakfast at a later time than normal. I was thinking about what I needed to take to the table with me? I knew that I wanted a candle next to me as this helps me detect spirit, I also placed some crystals next to me. I placed an A3 sheet of paper half under the laptop and put a pen there. I also brought a deck of angel cards to the table just in case I needed any extra help. I cleared all the energy within my home by sageing and then waited a couple of hours. So it's time, with my heart pounding and my hands sweating I placed a pint of water in a glass next to me at the table, I detect movement of spirit the other side of me at the table and I press the call button. The lady answers, and I'm instantly feeling a lot of energy moving through my body. We exchange the normal pleasantries, hello, hello etc and then I get straight into it and say what can I help you with? The lady says that, she has never been alone and now for the first time she will be alone as her son is leaving for university and she's not sure what to do? She is a very strong and independent lady with her own business, but I guess she's not aware of how strong she really is. She's never had time to herself and on the course they keep wanting her to go inward to build upon her inner world but she's unsure about it. After years of not being alone I could tell she suffered from co-dependent behaviour and this had been a topic on our course. So I reassured her that her son will always be there and that you now have been given the space and time to finally after all these years get to know and understand yourself on a deeper level and really build upon your inner world. Fantastic she said, that's exactly what I needed to hear, I had thought about it but now that I've been told I feel better she said. I felt like I hadn't done anything at all apart from seeing what was in plain sight. It must have been because she had heard it from another person as deep down she really knew what was happening and what to do it was just a matter of facing it. I think a lot of us suffer from that, we know our own answer but to move into a new direction is uncomfortable but often very needed. I continued to chat a little more and asked if there was anything else she needed but she said that was really the only thing. So after all my panic it really was a gentle first experience, I felt very fortunate and a little confused so I decided to go and research what Psychic meant.

Psychic: a person who claims to use extrasensory perception to identify information hidden from the normal senses. Psychics provide advice and counsel to clients.

I thought to myself, did I really use some special power? I know that I had a large amount of energy going through me the entire time that I was connected and that I was being guided by spirit but did I really just use all of my gift? I did counsel her I thought ? Ok let's not be hard on myself it is what it is, I fully helped the lady out and she was extremely pleased with the outcome so that's that.

My next client wanted me to do the reading over facetime call on the iPhone, no problem I can do that I said and booked him in. I did all the same preparations as before. I got ready and spirit was with me the other side of the table in front of me. I dialled and received no answer, so I called again and still no answer. So I sent out a text to ask if everything is alright. He responds saying his facetime doesn't work and that he thinks it might be because he has no internet at home? can I do it over the phone. Lucky for me I had already done it over the phone thanks to my friend. So I called him up. As soon as he answered all this energy was gushing through me again, like a current being connected to its source. Straight away I ask him what is the question he has for me? He tells me he has no question and he just wants to talk, so I said ok what would you like to talk about? He says he is in trouble at work at the minute and he's suspended. Words jumped out of my mouth completely uncontrolled and I said out loud "gross misconduct"! he was taken aback by it and I apologised straight away. For some reason I knew that I was right with my answer but he didn't want to talk about it. He rambled on about complete nonsense and I was beginning to get frustrated but tried to guide him here and there within these ramblings. I tried to get him to talk about work as I felt that is what he really wanted to talk to me about as he wanted to know the outcome but he wouldn't go there. I knew that gross misconduct was a sack able offence and that he would need hard evidence to fight against his appeal. As he said to me that he didn't want to talk about work the words jumped out of my mouth again "gross misconduct"! I apologised again and then let him ramble on at me for some time, an hour and forty five minutes later I finally gave in and said that I needed to go now. Once I hung the phone up the energy slowed in my body and returned to normal. I couldn't believe it that somehow I was forced to shout gross misconduct at him twice completely uncontrolled, almost like someone spoke through me. I felt very rude and also gutted that he didn't have a proper question for me and just wasted my time. Over the next few days I started to doubt myself and whether I was making the right decisions or not.

My next client was a lady that wanted to connect over iPhone video call. I did all the usual things to prepare, I saged my home and had my candles laid out. Just before the call the energy was moving very quickly through me again and I detected spirit the other side of the table as normal. Here we go I thought, I dialled the number and she answered straight away. She was a very lively person and seemed very positive from the start. She had a question for me, her question was " there's a guy at her works who used to talk to her all the time and this guy was very work confident. She warned him that his confidence would get him into trouble and sure enough he eventually got fired. From that point on he hadn't contacted her at all and she wanted to know why and what to do"? She was concerned as her life was dramatically improving. She was always coming to people's rescue which in turn used to sabotage her own path.

So first off I said, it might have shocked him as you were right about his behaviour getting him in trouble. Next thing is his confidence will have been knocked as he was very sure of himself. Also he might not have contacted for three reasons, he has no money to pay his phone bill so he cannot contact. He is hiding at home licking his wounds and as he has been left red faced. He has moved on and doesn't want to look back.

She hadn't thought of any of these as she had taken it personally and just assumed it was all her fault and had been carrying around that blame on her shoulders. Sometimes when you are an open person that is led by your heart you end up taking other people's actions as a direct assault against you. However once you begin to look beyond the self there in lies the answers.

So she wondered what to do as for her, her life was in fact going very well, she's had to work at this and now her work is paying off. She expressed past concerns that normally her life derails when she puts another person back on their tracks and she really didn't want that life anymore. I advised her that the reason that this situation has come up in her life was in fact a test, a test to see if you will accept your own growth. She hesitated and then decided to continue on her own path. She had recently gone for a job interview and when she told me about this my guides told me that she would in fact get the new job. I believed it was all resting upon this rescue outcome. They wanted her to change her old rescue patterns and focus on her own growth and the new job was the direction in which they wanted her to move in. She did in fact get the new job and her life is continuing to move forward in a positive direction.

This reading had been perfect for me as I heard my intuition loud and clear and was now back on track and confident again.

Next reading was over an email, this was a test for sure! So I had agreed I would give it a go. The email was from a lady and she asked, was now the right time for a relationship or should she focus on her career? I read the email about six times and my guides kept telling me it was a yes to relationship. I wanted to check check and double check so I decided to go and ask my angel card deck. As I sat there shuffling my cards I kept asking the question, I knew I was being channelled as I could feel it. I shuffled and a card literally jumped up out of the deck and landed face down on the ground. I put the pack down knowing that this card was the answer, I picked the card up and turned it over and it said "romance" wow I thought this is truly amazing! So without any further hesitation I emailed the lady back and told her that now was in fact a great time to find love and that love will find her.

I then learned that it doesn't matter whether it's a phone call, a text message, an email, a video call, as long as the connection has been made between me and the client then I can accurately give the answer. I decided it was now time to widely advertise myself.

Now over the years I have been through a lot of stuff and this has taught me a lot and given me more success in what I now do. Unaware that I was being spiritually guided I've counselled lots of people, given lots of guidance and lots of practical solutions to overcome addiction, depression, self-harm, anxiety etc and I decided that I would include this within my work. So the list was to be Energy clearing, Counselling, Readings. I decided to get business cards and flyers printed up. I took to the streets in my local town and attempted to hand out my flyers, my reception wasn't welcomed. Over the next few months I didn't receive any phone calls or bookings at all, doubt started to creep in again. My guides took over and channelled me into writing this book.

Over the next few months my guides had decided to channel me into writing two more books and to continue a long my spiritual path. One of the books was a children's book called The Adventures of Zak and Baby Grace. I worked nonstop on the children's book doing all the drawings myself and after some time I sent it off to the publishers and secured myself another contract.

I received the news that a friend of mine had been diagnosed with cancer and I remembered that some time ago I detected an energy block within him due to the non-grieving of his mother's passing. I had tried to meet up with him on several occasions but he was being a slippery customer, my intuition was telling me that he was avoiding me, maybe subconsciously he knew what was wrong. When I received this news about his cancer his partner wanted me to help him, so sure enough we began talking on the phone again. He wanted to know about treating his cancer with cannabis which in the UK cannabis is still illegal. I found some information on CBD treatment and also told him about meditation and how I thought that energy blocks could manifest into illness. I said that maybe we should meet up to have a better talk and so it was. Him and his partner were due to arrive at mine, on the day I was a little on edge as I knew he had a block that needed releasing and wondered if a message from spirit was going to come through. They turned up at mine and we did the normal hello's and then sat down on the sofa and began to talk straight away. Now I can't remember the conversation as I was taken over and channelled. I do remember him saying something about his father who had just passed away, I think he thought he hadn't grieved properly for him? But within that moment his mother came through and I could feel this ball of energy inside him on the move and as it was moving I told him the block is due to him not grieving for his mother and with that his body tensed almost like he had been punched and this ball of energy went up and out of his body which moved him to tears. I was correct that he hadn't grieved for his mother and he confirmed this and then explained that he had buried it down in his system. We talked for a long time afterward and his mother was channelling me the entire time. We cleared up some issues around his childhood that had been affecting him in his adult life. His mother thanked me and so did the angels. To this day he still cannot work out what I did or how I did it. Truth is it wasn't me, it just happens through me, it's his mum who healed him.

I had started an Instagram page a few years ago and I used to share some great photos of what people had taken as they travel the world. I found my posts changing as I was changing, I was now making my own posts that would help and inspire other people to live a better more spiritually minded life, I was becoming a light worker. I also set up an internet page promoting my work and found myself aiming more towards the spiritual counselling side of it, I advertised this web page on my Instagram page - www.instagram.com/russell0000000.

This lady was brought to my attention when I noticed a pattern of her liking a lot of these posts that I was making. One evening she had private messaged me asking if I do readings, I explained to her what I was about as I didn't want her feeling misleaded. She agreed that she wanted to connect so we arranged a time and connected over Skype as she lived in California. She was a very nice lady in her fifties. She began to have trouble understanding me and she asked if I would please talk slower due to my accent. So how are we going to do this she asked, are you going to use cards and give me a tarot card reading? Nope I don't do cards I said, I have angel cards for some straightforward questions but mostly if you have any problems or need guidance then tell me. Oh ok she said, so she paused for a second and then sure enough she said well... there is this one thing, yep go on hit me with it I said. Boom she had relationship problems and needed guidance and healing. She was separated at this time, staying in non-ideal accommodation, feeling worthless, hopeless, confused, betrayed, and unloved. We successfully moved through all issues and she grieved a lot which is good as that's part of the healing process. I gave advice in how to move forward, made her aware of her own power, and I gave her some instructions about how to move forward to and write this down during the video call. This was a massive step for her and after the initial session I checked in for the next few days to see how she was getting on. Healing is a big process and at these moments when we allow ourselves to be fully open we feel vulnerable, I consider it part of my job to check in afterwards in order for you to then not feel ashamed that you allowed yourself to become vulnerable around me. You see if you then allow yourself to feel ashamed you then open the door to negative thinking which in turn will then encourage negative feeling and then you are back where you started again. A true healer should never encourage co-dependent behaviour but at the same time they shouldn't open you up and then leave you high and dry.

During this time me and my partner welcomed in a new baby, this time it was a beautiful baby girl. We had decided to call her Grace Gladys Glennis Wilson; she was named after all the nans. Nana Grace had died a few years before but had decided to give me a visitation a few months after baby Grace had arrived. It's been a very busy time in my life, but as my grandad said, it's all going to get better. You know what, it actually has. I've had to work for it but it's all been worth it.

Spiritually I'm still learning and growing every day. I have worked hard and followed all of Heidi's instructions and I can honestly say that it has made a huge difference in my life. I'm in control of not controlling what comes at me. In myself I am centred and connected to everything in a peaceful way. I am still sensing spirits and following the path of my spirit guides. I have read books that I have received from Hay House books by Doreen Virtue, Wayne Dyer. Videos by Iyanla Vanzant, James van Praagh and my life is so much richer for this. It's because of all of these lovely people that I decided to take my nana's advice and write this book.